Speak Your Truth

Written by Michael Codrington

Acknowledgements
To my siblings, Candace, Edwin, Alwin, and
Sabrina. To my father Edwin Codrington. To Brian
Mooney, Maya Osborne, Christine Holm, Johanna
Lane, Sam Lagasse, Nick Muccio, and Ally Young.
To Henry Ross, Gabby Record, Gwyneth Atkinson,
and my beautiful mother Sybil Codrington. Last but
certainly not least, to the late great Daniel Perreault
Nakajima, Rest in Power Frequent Flyer.

Foreword

My book "Speak Your Truth" is about doing just
that. This past year was by far the worst year of my
life, and the subject matter of some of my poetry
reflects that. The book is also appropriately named
such because my senior year of high school truly
put me through the ringer. From dealing with toxic
people, to two of my good friends committing
suicide, there was never a moment of peace in sight.
What kept me sane was remaining grounded in my
identity. It was understanding what my own
personal truths were, and in turn projecting those
truths onto the rest of the world. The majority of
these works were written or finished in the past year
with a few exceptions. My work is brutally honest,
no holds barred.

      After watching the works of great slam
poets such as Rudy Francisco, Maya Osbourne,
Mahogany Browne, Sarah Kay, Dakoury Godo-
Solo, and Steven Willis, I decided that there was a
voice of spoken word lodged between my prose and
my contemporary poet. So, I tried my hand at slam
poetry at many open readings at The Putney School
summer arts program, where I really began writing
seriously.

      I also credit my inspiration and my style to
the music that I listen to. From the flows of Jay-Z
and Kendrick Lamar, to the grace of SZA and
Queen (surprising, I know!), I've been influenced
by every one of them.

      I hope you enjoy the piece of myself that
I've been able to share with you all. Enjoy!

Ghazal 1

The tears are talking again tonight
staining this page, as expected.

I see you're strumming on my
Heart strings, as expected.

My eyes are telling the truth
Red, bloodshot and blinking, as expected.

Each tear encapsulates
Sentiments of a shot untaken, as expected.

Part of me is happy,
However small, as expected.

I've spent too much time,
On forgone conclusions, as expected.

Tired is not the a suitable
enough word, as expected.

What I did not expect,
Was the bullet
The emotion that's leaving me
With a dropped jaw and a hole
Beneath the left side of my chest.

No Strings Attached

We went at our own pace on borrowed time,
Your kisses carry a new kind of love
Previously unshared between us.

Your bones were cold.
My fingers trace each vein on your arm
Curious about the ramifications of this decision.

All the sounds of the night,
were drowned out for 2 unconscious hours
by the TV that neither of us were watching.

The word love doesn't exist right now
Because it doesn't have to
Because we don't want it to.

If these walls could talk,
they'll tell me to slow down.
Grasp every moment now like it's
The last one we will have because it just might be.

I want to tell you
something that will mean something,
but I'd rather be happy with lies than
sad with the truth.

The fact that we will both willingly throw on our
masks
the same ones we've been wearing,
the same ones we've used to tear this down,
the first time.

The TV turns itself off,

We watch the sun come up together.

I had a dream that you and I were having dinner at a restaurant

I wasn't prepared for you.
You, dancing-diva,
you heaven-sent-heroine.

Inside my head,
I scream when you pass by me because,
The Hi! That I blurt out was supposed to be,

You're gorgeous.
That your laughter is sunshine in the form of sound
waves.
That your laugh is contagious and I have caught
your cold many times over.
That when you smile,
My brain tells the rest of my body
"Make her smile again".

You heart-breaker
Happiness- holder
You smile when I do stupid things because you
know they're simply tactics
Excuses to catch your eye.

You're... different.
I like different.

Post Traumatic Heartbreak Disorder

The worst pain
I've ever experienced was when I was 4
and after watching 2 hours of WWE
with my older brothers
I jumped off my bed
to give my pillow the people's elbow and broke my
collarbone
and almost died.

Not to be dramatic
I'd rather feel that again,
then find myself attached to another gamble of a
relationship.

A word
that causes my body physical discomfort by merely
being,
because the first time I fell in love
, I really fell.
hard.

I was 15 and that was the best time,
the beginning.
Making faces at one another for lack of anything
better to do,
wondering if she's thinking what you're thinking,
hoping she's thinking what you're thinking.
That was what I fell for.

The newness and the realness
I thought we were the realist
together and apart alike,
there was no one else I liked
or even looked at the way

my eyes fixated on her like each time it was the first
glance.
The first glance.
Or,
As I like to call it,
The first wave of vulnerability
Becoming extinguished.
Relationship is a strong word.
If I had known then what I know now
I'd just call it a mistake from the beginning.
The worst thing is I'm not mad, or resentful, just
confused.
If I could choose not to have fallen
in love I wouldn't which is
ridiculous and self destructive it's just that
when it was good it was great and when it wasn't I
felt how people feel when they take the SAT, or
when they're trying to make a flight. All the wrong
type of anxious.

My hands know
that the next time they will be held
I'll be back in that word
and I told myself I was done with this kind of thing
this,
attachment these
false promises that seem to seek me out tearing me
apart from the inside out.

But, the girl who broke my heart is not this girl who
I'm laughing with at lunch. So maybe it's not bad to
reattach, but I can't take that chance. I fear to
immortalize yet another person that has acquired
my attention.

But, there is the girl who I am laughing with at
lunch who finds a way to steal a smile from me
anytime she wants and
by that I mean
she makes me feel alive by having the recklessness
to revolt with a twinkle even when a day is
revolting .

If I were to be brutally honest with her at this lunch
table, I would let her know
how she is a seed in the forest after a fire,
hope.
I would let her know, that I have not eaten in the
last 15 minutes because I have been distracted,
that there is not another person that I would look
like a fool in front, which is just how I say I like
you.
How there were at least 5 different occasions
where I got really nervous trying to talk to her
for the first time and took a detour down the den
stairs instead
I know it'd sound weird but I'd tell her how she
makes me feel how I feel every time I watch
Muhammad Ali, at peace, like anything that I could
ever be is tangible because somehow you make it
so.
I'd say I'm sorry.

For the baggage I'm shouldering which is out of
your control
and before you,
I wish I could be something for you, girl
who makes me feel alive, girl
who found the key to my heart
even though I thought that I'd hid it better this time
girl

who I am laughing with at lunch.

Let's get dinner sometime.

Faith
Pursed between her puckered lips
are words you are drowning out
with words
she is all too accustomed
to shrugging off.

Because she knows
that she is your best kept secret,
no amount of gifts wrapped up with apology and
resentment will ever be sufficient.

Love sucks with a capital period.
You say between shared breaths under unneeded
covers.
Each fleeting second a microcosm for
The definition of your interactions.

Ghazal 2

A broken heart is what changes people
The sun still shines, the trees still grow.

Each shattered piece carries it's own story
The sun still shines, the trees still grow.

For some reason I can't stop it.
The sun still shines, the trees still grow.

Your piano keys sing when they dance
The sun still shines, the trees still grow.

Mine feel empty as I fantasize
The sun still shines the trees still grow.

Tomorrow, I will wake up as empty
As I would expect myself to,
Searching for what, I know I will not
find.
The sun still shines,
The trees still grow.

Unrequited Love

When I first met you
I was scared
Foot tapping, 2 seats away
Afraid I would slip up and say,
Your hair is amazing, that your eyes twinkle in the
moonlight
Instead, frozen, I just said hi.

You were so nice,
That made me anxious.
I wanted you to like me so bad
Your smile filled the room,
And my heart pounded out of my chest and
Into the palm of your hand,
A rhythm that only you could control now.

I'm not supposed to feel this way
That was never the plan.
Plans always change.
I used to make fun of you
Just so that I could say your name,
I would smile
But in my head just felt longing.
Give me my heart back.

10 ways to look at the woman you love

I
Through the glass pane
On a departing plane
As you go your separate ways
II
Her agony seems like it will never end
When she delivers your joint creation
As she suffocates your hand
III
First thing in the morning
She sneaks a grin out
Of the corner of her mouth
IIII
From the ground up
When you're hoping for a yes
And definitely not prepared for a no.
V
Hand on her stomach
To feel what she feels
Blossoming.
VI
Sitting adjacent in a restaurant
You knew she'd love
As the words
I love you
Slip from her tongue
VII
The sun is shining
She must be too
VIII
When she takes care of
Your sick behind
Making all the sacrifices
IX

When she's with you
After devastating news
and you believe
She'll always be there.
X
I do.
I do.
Fireworks.

Michael (Contrapuntal)

the artist,	The cool, the sweet
Identity is overrated.	But so hard to tackle
Pressure makes diamonds,	And you will shine
Try this on for size	Michael the Hurt
A loss is a lesson	learn before it's too late
Bent, but not broken	Scars are just proof of
How strong you are	who and what survived you
Michael the athlete	Wrestle with others
Compete all you want	Michael the Strong
Sorry, but one is not enough	Be all of the above.
And more,	

Ghazal 3

Because I have to, not by choice
There are ways of loving in secret.

And I have learned every one of them,
There are ways of loving in secret.

And ways of loving out loud
There are ways of loving in secret.

But I don't want to
There are ways of loving in secret.

But I can't keep my mouth closed
There are ways of loving in secret.

And I have learned everyone of them,
Not by choice, but because
There is simply no time for honesty when you're
somewhere you're not supposed to be.

I wanted to write a poem about someone else

Because often times the most important stories are

left untold.

I wanted to write a poem about someone else

because my pencil has no passion, without a knack

for empathy,

Even for those who did not always deserve it.

Because the people outside and in only judged her

outside and in her thick skin she felt

Hopeless.

Because her best friends have been killed

Their aspirations unfulfilled and hers... well we'll

get back to that...

Her depression told her the scale was in charge

That her pants were too tight because she was too

much.

It told her that the day was over before it would

start

and that it was her own fault that she was falling

apart.

Because after her father cheated on her mother they

separated half her life and to this day she still

questions if she is right, to question.

Because 2 times she was sexually assaulted and 2

times nobody believed her

And that boy thinks he did nothing wrong

Only assured himself a good time

The one who thought it was ok to take her

innocence and happiness and

Found it made sense to penetrate her defense and

attack her at a time of weakness.

Because every catcall calls for a recall of

confidence and self-esteem

until being happy

can only seem like a dream.

Because her learning ability

was slowed down by ADHD

And she began to see

That her brain worked differently.

Than you or me.

Because sometimes it's just too hard

And her scars remind her

Of how she was hurt.

And with knife to throat and head in hands

She tried to end the life that her mother and father

began.

When you see her

you wonder why she cannot lift her lips into

anything more than a frown

And you wonder why she shuts down

Well she was beat down

and put down

and sit down

and yelled at

She feels trapped

So just, don't

ask.

Scars

He was bigger.

Blood-stained hands, drip into a puddle,

Crooked fingers, headache pounding

"I can do this all day", but you can't

Raised voices, bear emotion, but

No tears because it feels all too familiar

This shouldn't be happening but no one can stop it.

Another blow.

The heat seems to intensify as you

Hit the ground again.

The puddle gets larger.

Your left eye is swollen shot.

This shouldn't be happening, but no one can stop it.

You get back up for the 4th time

But no intention of stopping until

you stay up, and he goes down.

Channeling your inner Ali, you cock back

Your right hook.

But even Ali lost sometimes.

Here and there

Here, when the moon shows itself, it brings with it

nocturnal night crawlers, tip-toe with precision.

Persimmon sweet is the howl of the evening breeze,

Time seems to freeze nightly, serenity.

There, clouds are forced to down airplane pills, in

the purple night sky dead or alive, never asleep,

bright lights serenade corneas tired feet pitter patter

on cement wet from sweat on your late night date

sirens blare holding a few dollars and a 25 cent

token.

Pressure
How much would I need, to do damage?
I can't manage, I am 17,
yet I have almost forgotten what it was like to be a
kid.
I have almost forgotten what it was like to be
carefree.
The obligation
to please my peers is what has brought me here.

Tears is too simple a punishment,
What have I done?
Where am I at?
No going back,
going numb.
Numbers onwards, lights backwards, stuck
same chapter,
same book.
I took a pill of some sort
at some point,
I don't want to disappoint but I already did. I
already did. I,
Cannot recognize myself in the cracked mirror, I,
Can't figure out how to turn the page,
How to fix this,
Can I fix this?

I can't, I'm livid,
I'm sitting, looking for
help I don't deserve
No words,
Screams, no sound
Now is the first time
That I've felt in the wrong place,
At the wrong time,
In the wrong skin.

Isn't that interesting to feel like you're in the wrong
skin?
but there's no incorrect way to own yourself.

Darius

I wish I had known you better. I was only 6, off-

brand white shoe Scooby-doo loving 6.

      That was my world.
      There were no guns in my world
      There was no death in my world.

We'd go over your house
Laugh on Saturday
Pray on Sunday
Nessy would make fun of my enormous head and
little body
I always wore my Dragon Ball Z shirt because it
was something we both loved.
You looked out for me all the time and I, I couldn't
even, muster the courage to say thanks or hi.
      Everybody cried. Especially Candace.
      The screams so many of us have to endure
      I was unsure of why, why
      Why was she screaming.

You were shot in cold blood by a man named Willie

Mays

"Black teen dead

Gang-related," the news headline read

We didn't know if you were in one,

But it didn't matter

People getting shot for the color of their boxers

For what they wear,

When and where they choose to be

By people who look like me.

Willie Mays, you killed my cousin and almost

killed 3 more

You are a monster, one I don't feel sorry for.

People talk about the hood

Like it's a fucking resort

And have no reason to care

About what's happening there

Because it's not happening to them.

How does a mother prepare

Her 2 boys and 2girls

To survive in this world,

The world,

That took you.

Darius, I can't write a fucking happy poem

Because all the dead boys look like you and me

How can I be optimistic

When everyday I fear of becoming a statistic.

Ballistic, I'm scared and afraid

Paranoid of the way

I walk, talk, even breathe

Because they'll kill me like they killed you.

Darius Jenkins,

I loved you,

I want to hit rewind and go back to happier times.

I wish I could see you today,

A couple days ago you would've been 27

And you would've been 5x any man.

I miss you and I wish I'd never had a reason to cry.

I wish you could see me now.

I wish I was still 6.

Land of the Free

Colin Kapernick is currently unemployed. That boy
passed for over 2,000 yards in very limited time,
holds the record for rushing yards for a quarterback
in playoff time(181) and played in that super bowl
game where the stadium lost power and he lost. But
he did lose to Joe Flacco who was on his way to
breaking the 23 year old record held by Joe
Montana for most touchdowns without an
interception in the playoffs but whatever.

Colin Kapernick is currently unemployed. And I
want to say that it's because he's black. But, it's not
just that, I mean the NFL is 68 percent brothers so it
can't just be his skin color it's, it's something more.
Probably because he kneeled for what you stood for
but let's backtrack. The American flag is the most
sacred but Kap claimed it represents hatred,

oppression, a sign of weapons of mass destruction,

destroying the "bad guys". The message is clear.

The American Flag should not be challenged.

Because it stirs unbalance and we'd rather all blame

him. But what if the Union didn't win? Would we

be pledging to the flag of the rebels, marveling at its

colors and history I don't know to me it's funny that

a guy on his knee is being taken down hard when

woman beaters and murders in the same league still

have jobs.

Not to mention sorry quarterbacks, Ryan Fitzpatrick

I'm looking at you. To the 30 owners, controllers of

America's favorite past time, you are saying hit our

women that's fine, but disrespect our flag and you

couldn't get another job if you tried. But why hate

on his silent battle cry, "I understand him but take

the flag out of it" oh because I'm sure other forms

of protest have been deemed effective, and between

you and me, if you think the 2 flags are that

different you might need a lesson in history. Every

time you praise that flag the invisible blood of our

enemies is upon it, yet we claim democracy, unity,

and peace but did we ever really want it?

August 19, 2010

I can't remember the last time we talked
Not yelled
Hugged, not fought.
Somehow the 25 cent candles lasted
Throughout the night.

We waited for you until 2am
My tears that stain this page
Are the same ones that stained this
tablecloth
I put on a happy face for our abomination of
a camera.
But, my mask was poorly constructed
Because I cried myself to sleep.

I told myself you were out getting me a
present,
That you'd have a PlayStation under your
arm or something.

The next day, you showed up for her.
A little big for 7,
But still your little girl,
Unraveling a Barbie doll.
That worked on her
But I didn't want that or anything worse
Than to here the words,
I love you son.

2003

A picture does not say a thousand words.

A good one doesn't have to.

Hindsight is always 20/20,

honey mixed into throat coat tea,

bunny ear TV,

and a baby.

Another baby due in 3 months time,

our world is about to get a whole lot bigger,

pictures do not speak because if they did,

they would tell the truth.

My first baby tooth,

cannot be seen, between me

sucking my thumb

and pondering when my dad would be present in

one of these,

I was a bit busy at 3.

Youth shrouded in loss,

what is the cost of a

"good picture".

Fuck a good picture,

I just want,

a complete one.

Ode to Derrick Rose

I was 12 years old when I,

broke my older brothers new 2k game

on which Derrick Rose donned the cover.

The best player by a mile

at the time, the second

coming of his airness, the first

of his kind rose would drop dimes spin and jam

inside hit a buzzer beater all in one prime time

night.

He wore Chicago on his chest, a hometown hero

Rose grew from the concrete of 79th street, he

Was the MVP

the bulls had been missing, he

Was an artist at dribbling, twisting

Hitting the toughest of shots.

I was 14 years old when I,

Saw a wilted Rose

Unable to support his own weight

Or that of Chicago,

Any longer.

His days of being a human highlight reel,

An afterthought, he

Unlaced his bright red Adizeros

The hometown hero,

A hero no more, he

was an artist cleaning his brushes for the last time,

he

Was an artist.

Ask Me

First things first
Are you white?
Black
Transracial Maybe?
#AskRachel

Identity theft.
Transracial?
Don't flaunt
a spray tan and say
You're as black as
The roots band.
I'm light skinned she says
No Megan Good is light skinned
Malcolm X was light skinned

You are not black
You're white skinned
That's comical
A white lady
wants to be black
Why pretend to share our struggle?
why pretend to struggle at all?
Do you want to live in a world where
The "Protection" guns you down?
or
Where you are dehumanized for being brown?
She finds it appropriate to
appropriate blackness
posing as a black woman
fighting for the oppressed
while gaining access to prominence.

It's funny because you can pretend your music
makes you black

That you are "about that life"
that you think you're black
but the simple fact
is that everyone wants to be black
until it's time to *be* black.

She's a Chameleon
a flip flopper without a care
She knows that if her blackness gets too difficult
she can shed it as easily as she can flat iron her hair.
Say you're something you're not
but when shit hits the fan
You can demand
to take off your mask
and stop pretending to be black
You don't understand!
The trouble and the hardships that we've endured in
your America.
Wouldn't it be nice if those kids at that Texas pool
party could've
claimed whiteness?
Or if
Under Trayvon Martin's hood was a friendly
Caucasian grin, able to walk freely on any block at
any time, any moment.

You don't get, that blackness is not an external
costume, it is an identity.
No matter how dark or light you may be,
To be a Negro in this country and to be relatively
conscious is to be in a rage almost all the time,
To be black is to not be able to open a history book
and see a time where your people's struggle are
nonexistent
To be black is to have your mother educate you on
what to do when you see police before you can get

educated in a school building named after a slave
owner,
To be black is to be seen as a Nigger not a name,
as a statistic, not a face.

Ask me what it is like to be black
, Because I been that, I been through the ringer
all before 18,
yes because my skin is dark,
but my soul is darker,
a culture and identity that I was born with,
not something that I attained over time.

But,
Nice Try.

Untitled from Luis ask to buy this one

Something by Caroline DeMellia

Our relationship is like an oatmeal raisin cookie, thinking it's a chocolate chip cookie you reach out with glee, realizing it's not, your hand coils back with remorse. It feels good to stay in the blue. Not quite confused, you know there's more to it .You smile and you hug and laugh, but that smile is forced, the hug thin, the laugh empty. Staying in the blue is dangerous, the blue is not real. Teeter on the tightrope of the black, for that is what is truly liberating, not the chocolate chip cookie, but the oatmeal raisin.

South Africa

Birds pollinate our noses
With the infectious grace
Of serenity.
She walks the path of our future
Aided by the past.
I watch and wait
As calm as can be
Yet amazed at her outstanding beauty.

She stops in front of me
And I shed a single tear
Not one of sadness or joy
But one of excitement.
We lock eyes
To find ourselves within the other.

We trade souls.
"I'll love you forever"
"You're the best thing that's ever happened to me"

I lift the curtains
And am blown away.
Because the most beautiful thing in South Africa
Was not the wildlife
Or the land we danced on
But it was my wife.
It was my wife.

Love

Love is amazing

Love is what really makes the caged bird sing.

Love is butterflies and googly eyes.

Love is the warmth of the embrace from your favorite face, when love knocks you answer because you know love is your answer.

Love is emotion yet sparks other emotions, love is devotion.

Love is Ali boma ye love is your way love is my way.

Love is universal

Love is resiliency, love is memory

Love is with whoever it want be, each love has its own identity

Love rings the bell of happiness within your consciousness.

But honestly, wouldn't it be something if love changed everything like everyone says it does.

Just for a second

Where Trump wasn't president

Just

One

Second

snap

Just one second how is he winning Pennsylvania and Michigan?

New Hampshire, Wisconsin?

"it's the silent majority man,

I called it".

Silent majority I hear you loud and clear.

How interesting you choose to shut your eyes and ears when black lives get picked off so fast you woulda thought it was the Damn NBA draft.

Funny you say silent, but your Facebook fox news likes speak volumes.

Rolling your eyes when another black boy dies
because you know "the cop was innocent " is not
silence, nor indifference.
It's disgusting.
Saying you have a lack of trust in the electoral
college will not solve anything, Donald Trump
winning says less about him and more about us
Him saying the N word would only increase his
good luck
Fed up, Fucked up.
How can you sit there blasting your Toby Keith
claiming Trump will drain the swamp
When he only ran red because he knew they'd be
the easiest people to top.
It's funny because, you thought it was funny.
This time last year he predicted a win over Bernie
and Hillary,
He individually picked apart his own party,
O'Malley, Chris Christie and 17 other losers.
I can't say I'm surprised, I never was,
Racism has been prevalent since long before I was.
Dear white liberals
Hello allics
Did you share on Facebook for shares or because
you actually care?
While you're cooped up on your couch watching
Trevor Noah,
Digesting diet racism
Will your white tears drown out the black ones or
Will you be different than your conservative
counterparts?
In part to his winning was his percentage of white
women
What is it you seek?
More representation, a woman running the nation,
better jobs, more respect?

Obviously not you voted for the opposition
He spits on your vision and hardens the transition
from the Obama administration
You say this is an overreaction,
that you accept the results in a democracy well , the
same people who told me this are the same people
who called my president a monkey, who dismissed
his ability to win because of his melanin, who said
"not my president" in 2008 and haven't changed
their tune since, you, want me to accept that my
safety is not prioritized
His rhetoric is fear in disguise
Scared of a black face with brown eyes
Scared of my black face with brown eyes
Scared of my black face.

Ode to Spring

In Winter's last days of summer
She could still hear the leaves
Smacking the pavement.

The birds chirped a little less often,
The shorts disappeared slowly
Then all at once.

People were seldom happy to see her.
She constantly saw their disdain
Through sarcastic disposition.

She would give the Earth a coat of her own,
And go gayly along each day
As if it was her last.

But through it all,
Her parties were always full
And she would make it
To summer again.

52

Red and Black are the last things you see
Before you lose it all,
Or win it all,
Depends on if your poker face is a bluff
Or his is,

You think you're a king,
He thinks you're a joker
4 suits dance in the dealer's hands
As your vibrato refuses to leave you
Neither does his.

The gamblers of the roundtable
Know all too well what's at stake
But can only depend on your mistake
Or lady liberty herself

Stained with whisky,
Or gin, its all a blur really,
Your suits refuse to dance
Lady luck time

Another slides across green velvet into your
hand
All eyes are on you
But your mind is on lady luck
3...2...1...
Red and Black.

Red and Black.
The last things he'll see before he loses it
all.
Because I'm a master of disguise
And his cards are bleeding.

A royal flush couldn't help
This court jester
Why is he still smiling
Fine, I'm not backing down either

Even the dealer knows I'm a shoo-in
And these clowns know I don't lose
What is up with him?
Does he know something I don't?

He's got nothing,
Stop messing with me and fold already
My palms are sweaty?
Fine, so that's how it's gonna be

Another card for the winner
Thank you kind sir
Time to find out
Which one is the loser
3...2...1...
Fuck.

Cut from the same cloth

Both: Ebony and Ivory live together in perfect harmonyyyyyyy..
Let me tell you a story,
No me first,
No me first.
Henry: Ok, fine
Michael: Michael Codrington was born August 19, 2000. 4:56 am. In New York.
H: Henry Ross was born November 1, 1999, 1:32 pm. In New York.
B: Michael's dad was never home
B: Henry's mom was never home.
H: Home might be the wrong word, present is better.
M: The only present I really got from my father was our shelter. Me and my dad never saw eye to eye only fist to eye, I never realized that his "tough love" was...
B: Abuse from your parents isn't just physical.
H: It's mental. I've never seen my creator's eyes bear such fire, what do you desire at the end of this fight, at the culmination of you beating me down...
B: Inside
H:My brain bruises
M: But outside my body does. My little sister watched me take the beatings, needing an explanation, looking for a reason that her brother was in...
B: Pain
H: Which I went through by myself my subconscious is irreparably calloused from your callow tyrades about god knows why today,
M: Luckily for me, you mostly missed. But when you didn't you didn't. You aimed for my face but

what you did was burn the invisible bridge that makes this what it is.

B: *My wounds both seen and hidden demand to be felt.*

H: How do you think I felt when you shoved a letter opener into my hand, demanding me to take your life because that's what I wanted? You dead, right? And There's no poetic way to say that.

M:How do you think I felt when I found out about my brother? Why his mom was different, why he even existed? I was 6 when I found out you actually had 4 kids. 6 whole years without my brother Alwin because you were scared to admit the truth. And there's no poetic way to say that.

B: *I am who I am because of my past but*

H: I was built to last.

M:I was built to last.

B: *I was built to last.*

H: What hurts most is my bad memories have become

B: *baggage*

M:Getting heavier with every stressed syllable, the pinnacle of my childhood has blood splattered on it from our bouts.

B: *My testimony falls on deaf ears because I am a kid, and you are an "adult. I'm only (16-M 17-H) but my mind is older because it has to be*

H: I feel like a seasoned veteran in a 17 year olds body. I'll say I'm sorry, but the thing is, I'm not when you're mom's a lawyer there's no use calling the cops.

B: *To my brother*

M:Stay strong, I know it feels wrong to be the bigger man when your fathers in the next room, but you have to.

B: *To my brother*

H:You've made me man of the house by default, I don't consider you family we just occupy the same space, I tell people I'm an only child because it's easier than the truth, the memories of my youth are pockmarked by you.

B:I'm always making jokes because laughter is my distraction

H: The laughs I produce are devices to silence the voice inside that says you were right.

M: That I am wrong, no amount of forced smiles I plaster on can make me forget.

B: Believe me I've tried.

M: Your reaction to me crying because you missed my middle school graduation was to "man up" but it's been 4 years and I finally know I was more than man enough.

H: Ours was the last bridge you had left intact.

B: Day after day you chip away, take what I have and what sucks is I'll stay.

M:If you said you were proud of me just once, this poem might not exist.

H:You insist that I'm the problem but look in the mirror,

B: It's not me, it's you

B: And all of me wishes that wasn't true because...

B: I love you

Ode to That Night
I wonder if,
in those 20 minutes,
you pondered assignments you knew you would
never turn in, the teachers
taking attendance the next day,
unaware that you would not be sitting right there
as you always were.

I wonder if,

you listened to the silence,
echoed by the soft breeze
flowing in and out of the tracks
on that cool September night.

I was in the library when word broke.
Choked with tears, someone told me it was
someone,
But not you.
Just a boy, from Andover.

Our last time
was at breakfast.
That same morning I could've said something
To let you know,
I'm here.

I wonder, if you just wanted to disappear,
Not die.
Had you tried, before this?

Pronounced dead at 7:26
Unbelievable, unpredictable.
This,

A tragedy, a mystery,
with no answer.
I called, somehow expecting you to answer.

Did you imagine an afterlife?
Did you have plans to be home in time for your
mom's famous cooking?
Did you wonder if you would even be recognizable,
afterward,
if there was an afterward?

Did your mind move backward,
your life flashing,
the train flashing,
your life flashing,
passing only the most important moments.

I hope I was in there,
but that's selfish and so is this poem,
I should be happy if you're happy, right?
I wonder,

if you found what you were looking for,
If you live in the rain and thunder,
the sun, the stars.

Did you follow a particular trail to your swan song
or
did you walk aimlessly.
Did you even want to feel alive?

I wonder,
If the people on the train thought
you were just a dumb kid,
if it was an accident,
If they would make it home that night,

If you would make it home that night.

I wonder
If I could have helped.
But that is selfish, and so is this poem.

Metamorphosis

The first time I can remember,
Was at summer camp when I was only 8.
Or 9 maybe, I guess you could say I was apart of
Camp Walden's affirmative action,
They had me, Elijah, Erick, Jarrett, and 500 white
kids, so what was I to do,
But to try to blend in, to contain my blackness in the
suitcase that I brought with me,
And store it away until it was time to leave.
Store it away except for the times where they
needed someone who was street to oversee their
appropriation of my own culture.

I was 9 when I compromised who I was for the first
time,
when I tried to stop being black for some sort of
prominence
for some sort of acknowledgement from my white
counterparts.
In 4 weeks, I had somehow believed that
the "ghetto" parts of myself were not to be desired
and
in turn that I,
was not to be desired.
How susceptible to newness we are in adolescence,
never tired of ideas and thoughts,
Unskeptical of unfathomable self-loathing.

Why did I stand in the mirror
Trying to brush my hair to get it to look straight,
reaching for the unattainable?
Why did I, simply accept that
what they were saying must've been correct,

that the way I talked was incorrect?
That my Bed- Stuy vernacular was tainted?

It's funny how people have a way of
making you think that by choosing to be yourself
you're missing out on something better, but you can
never go wrong with being yourself.
Not "respectable".
There is nothing respectable in being respectable,
be extraordinary be limitless raise fists raise hell
black prince because
lord knows our lives are too short
To waste them coloring in between the lines,
and by the way there's nothing funny about the N-
word
so slap a white boy if he wants to try you today and
say to him,
That is not yours.
I know that it's not something you're used to
hearing.

Black man,
you have a copious amount of culture at your
fingertips
Be careful because you are dripping in it,
Even in your walk
When a black man walks,
His feet slap the pavement with black boy joy
A jive on the 2 and 4 never the 1 and 3
1 in 3 of us is "supposed to be" in jail
But those numbers have never seen brothers like us.
Black man,
Know that every time you succeed,
That you're not supposed to be there
Because, they are afraid.

Every day,
every second
every minute
spent advancing, enhancing, improving yourself
someone will find a problem with it,
but they'll put on a smile,
it's something they won't admit that
they know in my flow in my rhythm, my blues my
truth, that
all black boys are born with wings.

Each one of us black men can fly,
easy too, second nature
like riding a bike.
Black man,
You are not anyone's token,
Be fearless be outspoken
It's important to stretch those wings
It's ok if you lose a couple of friends on the way.
Friends come and go,
But a brother is permanent.

Be your brother's keeper
Linked arms through life
Standing side by side,
Marching
On the 2 and 4
I see it
Black souls galore
With kinks and coils and fros and blowouts
Flat Tops and dreadlocks
Beautiful black power
Black Man, you are beautiful.
Black Power.

Curtain
Don't take this
the wrong way.
But,
My background on my phone
is us.

But, I'm barely
in the photo
it's you.
More specifically, your smile.

As you're retreating,
Fleeting from the spotlight
As you often do
Humble, yet harmonious with heaven
The flash catching you
At the last possible moment.

Mortified rosy cheeks for
Concern of looking pompous.
This is my background because
It's said
That the perfect picture does not exist.

And I want to be sure
My proof is prepared.
Right There.

I'm Working on my Ego

If you didn't know me all that well,
you might think I'm a little bit in love with myself. I
mean,
why the fuck not?

Who have you ever seen make 17 look this clean I
mean,
not to toot my own horn but...
nah never mind Imma do it to 'em.

I'm probably the funniest person I know,
I was the 6th member of the fab five,
the 5th member of the fantastic four, I am so fresh
and so clean that Andre 3000 himself would be in
awe.

Did I mention I'm the smoothest?
When I play jenga the pieces slide out for me
I'm just. that. nice.
My hands were carefully crafted by God herself,
Sealed inside each finger is a dash of swagger,
so much so that everything I touch turns to gold,
I got that Midas touch baby!

Yes, I am the one you've been looking for, your
savior,
the trap lord, Shaolin Fantastic, The greatest, The
prettiest,
I am the greatest, I am the greatest, I am the
greatest, I am...
working on my ego.

And I'd like to say that the overt overconfidence is
legit

but you've been punk'd
no Ashton Kutcher though this is the black version.

None of us are exactly who we say we are and I am
no exception,
accepting that my appearance will always be met
with some sort of tension because I look
"menacing" and "intimidating" is a hard pill to
swallow.
I'm working on my ego because everyday I pray for
clean arms,
tracing my not so discrete scars,
reminders of the last time I felt truly defeated.
Of the things that I've needed in my life
none has been more important than love from my
father.
Why do I bother after 17 years to look for a
diamond of love in an abusive rough?
I love you is all you had to say, or a hug or
something I don't know.
My ego is not impenetrable.
As a matter of fact, it's quite the opposite.

But I'm working on it.

To my brother on your 20th birthday

I see you.

We are 9 and 11 on Christmas day,
right before the fight of our lives,
snickering amidst our bickering
tensions flare as tempers rise,
that was not the first time nor would it be
The last, of our bouts.

We are 14 and 16, on the summer solstice,
I remember it like clockwork
and you stopped me and our father
from getting into it,
a peacekeeper if one ever did exist.

We are 16 and 18,
Yet on move-in day,
your orientation leaders congratulate me
instead of you, to which
you simply shrug and chuckle.

Today,
We are 17 and 20.
And still,
you are able to make me feel like a kid
precisely when I need to.

Brother, I see you carrying the weight of a
last name and aspirations, understand
this: no matter when your last birthday is,
no matter what you do from then until
now,
I will be unable to see you as anything
other than my big brother ,

who makes me feel like a kid,
precisely when I need to.

Hello again! Hopefully if you're reading this you've gotten through Speak your Truth from cover to cover and for that, I thank you. Working on this project over the last few years and especially the last few months has been exponentially rewarding. I thought that you might like to know a little bit about who you're actually reading.

My name is Michael Codrington and I was born August 19,2000, as mentioned in Cut from the Same Cloth, and eluded to in August 19, 2010. I've always been an absolute goofball, and one of the younger ones amongst my friends. For all of elementary and middle school, I attended

Excellence Boys Charter School in Bed-Stuy. After excelling in school, I was exposed to a few different life-changing opportunities. From Johns Hopkins CTY, to Prep for Prep, to the Jack Kent Cooke Foundation, to finally Andover.

I recently graduated from the prestigious Phillips Academy, a top boarding school in Massachusetts, which became my home in many different ways. I can recount endless memories and experiences that, had they not happened, I would not be who I am to this day. Though you can often find me joking around, I'd actually describe myself as shy in many aspects.

I'm a freshman at Howard University, or as I like to call it, The Mecca. Howard became the clear choice for me in the middle of April and it manifests a culture that makes me excited about writing, something that I haven't felt since attending the Putney School Summer Programs, which is where I really started. I'll be studying both English and theater there for the next few years.

My next steps after Speak Your Truth, include a book that details the events of my senior year as a black face in a white place. I talk about the many different masks that I've had to put on, the different experiences that shaped my behavior and personality, and overall what it was like going to Phillips Academy. The book is called Many Hats, Many Masks, and I am very excited to get it out into the world sooner rather than later.

My interests include Football, Basketball, Track and Field, Singing, Acting, journaling, and going on adventures. I hope that this book is just the beginning for me, and that I will write more books, whether they be poetry or not. In the future, I also hope to utilize my degree to tell the stories of those who have silenced voices. It's something that I've always been about. I hope you had half as much fun reading as I had writing, because I had a ball.

Made in the USA
Monee, IL
23 August 2020